FINLAND

THE LAND OF A THOUSAND LAKES

Distributed by:

Papermark

Pikku-Parolantie 6
13100 HÄMEENLINNA
FINLAND

CENTRO STAMPA EDITORIALE
plurigraf
PERSEUS

Original Text: *Stefania Belloni*
English Text: *Prof. Brian Williams*

Sincere thanks to the *Finnish Tourist Board of Milan* and the *Finnish Tourist Board of Helsinki* for their kind collaboration in the production
of this book and for permission to use the photographs listed below.

Photographs:
Giovanna Dal Magro: pages 76, 79/1.
Franco Figari: pages 1, 2, 4, 5, 17/1, 18/1, 19, 24, 24-25, 30, 31/1, 31/2, 32, 33/1, 33/2, 34, 36/2, 36/3, 37/1, 43, 44, 45/1, 45/2, 46, 47, 48,
51, 59, 60, 61, 62/1, 62/2, 63, 64/1, 67, 71/2, 74, 75, 77/2, 87/1, 88, 90/2, 91.
Finnish Tourist Board (Helsinki): pages 16 (Auset) – 18/2, 70/1, 71/1, 71/3 (M. Tirri) – 22/2, 26 (L. Lawson) – 27/1, 65 (E. Jämsä) – 38 (Foto-Prima)
49 (F. Widler) – 50 (P. Lempiäinen) – 52 (A. Aaltonen) – 53/1 (T. Karvimen) – 53/2 (T. Kanerva) – 58 (M. Varjo) – 68 (P. Nieminen) – 87/2 (Fotoplan).
Finnish Tourist Board (Milan): pages 7 (J. Hukka) – 11, 13, 14 (M. Tirri) – 15 (Q-Studio).
Cesare Gerolimetto: pages 6, 8/1, 10, 20, 54/1, 54/2, 55, 78, 79/2, 80/1, 80/2, 81, 82, 84, 85/1, 85/2, 89/1, 90/1.
Jari Halminen: pages 83/1, 93.
Heureka: page 22/1.
Mauro Parmesani: pages 9, 27/2, 28, 37/2, 41.
Esko Pärssinen: page 92.
Plurigraf Archive: page 86.
Hannu Vallas: page 64/2.
Markku Wiik: front cover, pages 3/1, 3/2, 3/3, 3/4, 8/2, 12/1, 12/2, 17/2, 23/2, 29, 35, 36/1, 39, 40/1, 40/2, 40/3, 42, 56-57, 66, 69, 70/2, 72-73, 77/1, 83/2, 89/2, 94, 95.

The publisher apologizes in advance for any unintentional omissions and would be pleased to insert appropriate acknowledgements
in any subsequent edition of this publication if advised by copyright holders.

© Copyright by
CASA EDITRICE PERSEUS - PLURIGRAF collection
Published and printed by:
Centro Stampa Editoriale Bonechi,
Sesto Fiorentino (FI)

Contents

Introduction

Each year, many of the tourists who choose to visit northern Europe pass through Finland on their way to the mythical Nordkapp, the most northerly point of the European continent.

During this long voyage, many of them perhaps forget to pay much attention to the seemingly endless landscape which accompanies them visually right up to the last moment, so great is their anxiety to reach their legendary destination. These vast stretches of woodland and forest form a landscape which in fact would take our breath away, could we see it from above. However, there are not many mountain ranges from which we can gaze out over this view, embracing thousands and thousands of lakes, an incalculable number of small islets covered with pines, firs and birches, winding, untamed waterways which force their way between cliffs, pinewoods and birch forests. Here the roads have to follow the edges of the lakes, and cross the waterways at the narrowest point. There are plenty of panoramic routes, but the best way to discover Finland is undoubtedly to bury oneself in its luxuriant and unspoilt natural endowment on foot or by bicycle, giving oneself the chance to make contact with this wonderfully evocative countryside.

Consider the Finns themselves: from childhood onwards they become used to living in close harmony with their rich natural surroundings, and for the people of this country, respect for this priceless and irreplaceable gift is the only way to enjoy a real relationship with the environment in which they live.

So try to become a little Finnish

4

yourself: sit down on the shores of a lake to fish enveloped in unbroken silence, except for the bird-song. Or take a walk in the woods in search of wild mushrooms or blueberries, to get used to the calm of this new rhythm of life, more suited to the real needs of humanity. Follow the winding routes of the pathways which cross the woods and forests and numerous national parks, without the pressure of haste.

If you have a more adventurous temperament, you can venture in a canoe on to the wild rapids of the rushing streams, or sail along the southern coast discovering the thousands of lonely islands of the southern archipelago or the Åland group. In the evening, on the banks of the lake, there will be a revitalizing sauna awaiting you, and it will be one of the most relaxing experiences you could ever have.

Apart from the countless natural and scenic beauties, Finland has a great cultural heritage to offer the visitor. Little towns with ancient centres perfumed by the wood of their houses, cities important in history, which host cultural events of the first order; fine ports along the coast, ancient and romantic communities which still keep intact their love of craftsmanship and the carving of their best-loved material, wood. And many villages where the joie de vivre still keeps alive ancient cultural traditions.

Finland is all this and much else: it is nature at close quarters, and a quite extraordinary way of life.

If we really manage to attain the spirit of absolute union with nature which inspires the people of Finland, that spirit will remain with us as an indelible memory, an experience beyond price.

HELSINKI: WHITE CAPITAL OF THE BALTIC.

On 12th June 1550, during the period of Swedish domination, orders were given by Gustavus Vasa that a port city should be built on Finnish territory facing on to the Baltic. It had to be capable of competing with the other important port of the Swedish Empire, present-day Tallin in Estonia, which was then known as Reval.

This was how Helsinki, the city which would eventually become not only Finland's most important port, but also its capital, was founded. It began life on the delta of the River Vantaa, in a wild spot, covered with thick vegetation and constantly buffetted by the wind. Initially, it was a quiet township by the sea, engaged exclusively in trade, with its little wooden houses straggling along the rugged peninsula formed by the deposits from the river Vantaa. But later it became more and more active and busy, until eventually it took on the role of Finland's new capital, despite the fact that the city of Turku – the previous capital – had more inhabitants and a more flourishing economy.

The motives behind this were purely political: the decline of the Swedish empire at the beginning of the nineteenth century, and the subsequent annexation of Finland to Russia, made it necessary for the Finnish capital to move closer to St Petersburg, to allow the Russians greater political control over their newly-annexed territories. Thus the choice fell on Helsinki, and even today, Turku still recalls this episode with a certain degree of bitterness.

In all honesty it must be admitted that when Helsinki was chosen for the new seat of government, it hardly possessed the real characteristics of a capital city. The great fire of 1808, which had virtually destroyed it, had swept away almost all the most important public buildings.

For this reason, an immediate reconstruction plan was needed, and this was entrusted to Johan Albrecht Ehrenström, and carried out by the German architect Carl Ludwig Engel. The latter completed the rebuilding project in 1840, giving the city the neo-classical character which the old centre of the capital still keeps virtually intact, even today.

The more modern part of the city grew up after the second world war, but never without reminders that it represents a land where nature and greenery are the unchallenged masters. Woodlands, parks and waterways in fact occupy a great deal of the city's surface space, and the buildings which stand among them are blended harmoniously with the natural elements, never absent in a Finnish city.

The Central Station in Helsinki.

VISITING HELSINKI

For lovers of modern architecture, Helsinki is a Mecca. The city has grown outwards towards the sea, especially on the surrounding islands and peninsulas, but it has never given in to the easy appeal of tall buildings, typical of so many other cities. It has always retained its own individual building philosophy, a kind of model pattern made up of low buildings of human dimensions, in which great care has been taken over aesthetics, and which have been inserted with a sense of harmony into the variegated urban landscape.

Many of the buildings have been influenced by architectural masters such as Alvar Aalto, Eliel Saarinen, Hermann Gesellius, Armas Lindgren and S.J.Sirén, who have left their unmistakable imprint on the urban pattern of the city, Their stylistic message is still alive today, and is an important departure point for the planning of new buildings in the city.

Our visit to Helsinki begins with the **Central Station**, designed by Eliel Saarinen, and completed in 1914. This is perhaps the most famous of all Finnish architectural projects, clearly influenced by neo-Romantic forms, and today, with its integrated building structure and the geometric ornamentation of its main entrance, seen as a kind of symbol of the birth of modern Finnish national architecture, previously mainly conditioned by local traditions.

The contrast between the vertical sweep of the granite walls and the curving copper roofs, developed symmetrically in relation to the main entrance arch, is a masterly innovation in modern architecture, which succeeds in combining rationality and creative force in a completely original composition. The sides of the main entrance are marked out by four monumental

The Ateneum Museum, the most important of Finland's National Galleries.

torch-bearers, the work of the sculptor Emil Wikström.

Before leaving the main square, we should not miss a visit to the **Ateneum**, a museum in which the most important collection of national art is housed. It gives an overview of Finnish pictorial expression during the last two centuries, with an annex dedicated to the French and Flemish impressionists. The building which houses the

museum is itself an excellent example of late nineteenth century Finnish architecture.

The focal point of the monumental centre of Helsinki is the imposing Senate House Square, in the heart of the city. This square has exceptional breadth and unison in its architecture, still bearing faithful witness to the rebuilding project of the days when Helsinki was chosen as capital. The majority of build-

ings which face on to the square, and which form a rare example of stylistic continuity in such a broad spatial area, are by the architect Carl Ludwig Engel, who planned them in the neoclassical style which was to become the *leitmotif* of the whole reconstruction of Helsinki in the first part of the nineteenth century.

On the southern side is the oldest building in the square, the **Sederholm Residence** (1755-1757) – obviously built prior to the reconstruction, and left intact by Engel. On the west is the building of the **University of Helsinki**, moved to the capital from its original seat in Turku. Its splendid **University Library** is housed in the fine building near the Cathedral: the neo-classical reading-room is surmounted by high vaulted arches resting on Corinthian columns.

On the eastern side of the square is the **Government House**, which also contains the Ministry of Foreign Affairs.

On the north, the dominant form is the outline of the city's Lutheran Cathedral of St Nicholas. It is crowned with a fine central dome in copper, while the lower part is characterised on all four sides by the same pattern – a pronaos surmounted by a drum sustained by four columns. This is another of Engel's projects, completed in 1852.

The Lutheran Cathedral and the Monument to Czar Alexander II in Senate Square.

The Lutheran Cathedral.

THE CITY'S CHURCHES

Obviously, the Cathedral is not the only important church in the city. Helsinki has a large number of churches for all the main religious denominations. Among these is the Catholic Church of St Henry, patron saint of Finland. This was built in 1860; it is a small chapel, which stands in the Kaivopuisto Park.

There is also another cathedral, this time belonging to the Orthodox Rite. This is the **Uspensky Cathedral**, an attractive red brick building dating from 1868, which is in an elevated position on the little island of Katajanokka; it was designed by a Russian architect, A.M.Gornostayev.

Also among the more interesting religious buildings is the **Temppeliaukion kirkko** – the Church on the Rock – in the Töölö quarter. Outstandingly original in conception, it was built in 1969 to a design by Timo and Tuomo Suomalainen.

The dome of this Lutheran church consists of a spiral formed by threads of copper wire, and this is the only element of the church visible from the outside. The interior, based on a circular plan, was carved entirely out of the rock, and is structured like a Pantheon, with granite walls which provide a perfect echo for sounds, so that the church has become a favourite place for concerts.

The Uspensky Cathedral, seen from Helsinki Harbour.

The Temppeliaukion Church, carved out of the rock-face.

A VISIT TO THE MUSEUMS OF HELSINKI

In a country where there is such enthusiasm for reading, and where the cultural life is particularly lively, it comes as no surprise to find that there are so many museums in the capital. The variety and special interests of these museums is enough to satisfy curiosity of every kind and on every subject.

For lovers of painting, in addition to the Ateneum mentioned above, the obligatory visit is to the **National Museum**, which has a magnificent collection of international works of art, archaeological finds, objects and costumes in its numerous exhibition rooms, summing up a large part of the history and folklore of the country, including some finds dating from the Stone Age. The Museum itself is housed in a very fine building,

given an upward thrust by an elegant composite tower. It was designed by Saarinen in 1910, and is a fine example of the national romantic style.

The **Cygnaeus Gallery** also deserves a mention – a rich collection of nineteenth century paintings housed in a sober wooden building. There is also the **Gallén-Kallela Museum**, which possesses the works of one of Finland's most esteemed painters, displayed in a "Liberty" style building designed by the artist himself. Many interesting exhibitions of contemporary painters are also held here. Another fine collection of paintings, this time by foreign artists, is to be found in the Gallery of the **Sinebrychoff Academy of Finnish Art**, the largest collection in Finland of works by Italian and Flemish painters.

There are naturally many places dedicated to contemporary exhibit-

ions, such as the **City of Helsinki Museum of Art** or the **Tuomarinkylä Museum**.

For enthusiasts of Finnish architecture and design, Helsinki has two particularly interesting museums. One is the **Museum of Finnish Architecture**, a real shrine to visit in order to get to know more about Finland's highly original constructive creativity, which ranges from *national romanticism* (the most brilliant exponent of which was Eliel Saarinen), to the *classicism* of the 1920's, represented by Sirén. There are also many examples of subsequent stylistic trends such as the *functionalism* of Erik Bryggman, and of the masterly Alvar Aalto, the greatest name in modern Finnish architecture. Aalto is one of the most important innovators not only in the field of architecture, but also in that of town and regional planning, as well as in the sector of furnishings and applied art. The ex-

Finlandia Hall, the great centre for conferences and cultural events, designed by the architect Alvar Aalto.

hibition continues right up to the most modern and original stylistic trends, which lay stress on the malleability of materials and forms: in this area the greatest innovations have been achieved by the expressionism of the architectural couple, Reima and Raili Pietilä. Many of the projected ideas of these famous architects first saw the light of day in Helsinki: the city could thus be considered to be a sort of practical workshop of what is to be found in the museum. In this sense, one of the most notable buildings is unquestionably **Finlandia Hall**, where conferences and cultural events are held. It was built in the early seventies to a design by Alvar Aalto; covered in Carrara marble, it is a white, many-storeyed frontage broken up by tall, narrow openings, which provide a rhythmic variegation to the plain mass of the building. We continue our imaginary stroll through the vast open-air museum of architecture which is Helsinki: we find a fine example of the classicism of the third decade of this century in the **Parliament House**, an architectural masterpiece built at the end of the twenties, on the basis of a design by J.S.Sirén, which won the 1924 competition. Contemporary architecture is represented by the **Residence of the President of the Republic**, or **Mäntyniemi**, designed by Raili and Reima Pietilä and completed in 1993. It is only possible to mention a few of the dozens of buildings of architectural merit; on a thorough visit to the city one will find at least a hundred more which catch the eye and underline the impressively basic and sober character of Finnish architecture. To return now to the museums: the other essential visit for devotees of avantgarde design in contemporary objects is to the **Museum of Applied Art**, which provides a complete collection of refined and yet essentially simple Finnish design, applied to the greatest variety of objects and accessories in common use. Sports enthusiasts will find their interest

The Olympic Stadium - detail.

catered for by the **Finnish Sports Museum** in the Olympic Stadium, where all the most important names in Finnish athletics are represented. The Stadium complex itself, built for the Olympic Games in 1940, is a fine sight, surmounted by a tower over 220 feet high. If the visitor is a keen photographer, we suggest a visit to the **Finnish Photographic Museum** where each day temporary displays are mounted of all the most famous Finnish and foreign photographers. Stamp Collectors too can find their interest provided for in the **Postal Museum**, which often puts on unusual historical exhibitions on the subject of philately, and has an extensive collection of national and foreign postage stamps. For those who love the sea and navigation in general, on the islet of Hylkysaari there is the **Historical Museum of Navigation**, which has a large collection of boats on display directly in

the sea, as well as many scale models, numerous maps, and typical sea-going navigational apparatus. The ultra-modern **Museum of Contemporary Art**, **Kiasma**, has been designed with all types of visitors in mind. In addition to its collections of works which range from the 1960s to the present day, it hosts temporary exhibitions as well as having a theatre, an interactive information centre, a confernce room and guide facilities for both general and specific sections.

Finally there is also no shortage of unusual and original exhibitions like that of the **Museum of the History of Medicine and Surgery**, or the **Museum of Hotels and Restaurants**, or even that of the **Tram** – now housed in the city's oldest public-transport depot. In between museum visits, it may prove of interest to pay a call on the city zoo. This is to be found on the islet of **Korkeasaari**, which was

transformed into a zoological garden in 1889, and has fine examples of the wildest forms of Nordic fauna, such as reindeer, musk-ox, Siberian tigers and white leopards. If you have a taste for open-air museums, head for the islet of **Seurasaari, where an open-air Museum was created in 1906**. This can easily be reached on foot by using a passageway which takes the visitor on a journey back in time. More specifically, we return to the seventeenth and eighteenth centuries, the age when the majority of Finns lived in wooden houses (more than a hundred of which have been transferred here), or attended churches like that of **Karuna,** dating from 1685, in a very evocative country atmosphere. There are many characters to be seen around in typical costume in the summer, and visitors can take part in characteristic singing and folk-dancing.

Open-air museum on the island of Seurasaari.

Monument to the composer Jean Sibelius in the park dedicated to his memory.

NATURE WITHIN EASY REACH: HELSINKI'S PARKS

Another very pleasant activity in Helsinki is to take long, exhilarating walks around the numerous parks of the city, perfect gems nestling in the setting of its different quarters.

Each of them contains its own particular treasure: we find a museum in one, a church or a monument in another – as in **Sibelius Park**, for instance, where the famous composer's monument stands. Sibelius' monument is a remarkable and distinctive metal sculpture cast in 1967, the work of the sculptress Eila Hiltunen, whose work is certainly among the most outstanding expressions of contemporary Finnish art.

Another park of great beauty is **Kaivopuisto**, in the elegant residential southern part of the city; there is also the **Kallio**, a great stretch of green broken up by two small lakes. It houses the Civic Theatre and the City Administration Building, two more interesting examples of modern Finnish architecture.

Another of the capital's attractions is to be found in the open-air markets. There are many of them, all crowded and lively with colours, scents and shoppers. The biggest is the one which is held in the Market Place itself, known as **Kauppatori** in Finnish; it stands directly on the sea-front.

Something of everything is sold in the market: fruit, flowers, local handicraft products – a real paradise for tourists, especially on the fine days when the wind is not too strong. During the summer the market is open in the evenings as well, as is the flea-market to be found in the other market-place, **Hietalahti.**

The Market Place (Kauppatori).
Kiasma, the Museum of Contemporary Art.

Recently the National Park of Nuuksio has been opened in the environs of Helsinki. This is a protected area of app. 17 square kilometres with small pools of water, lakes and huge rocky outcrops, separated by fine strips of thickly-wooded countryside. There are many hikers' paths, and it is possible to catch sight of the park's symbolic animal - the Russian flying squirrel.

THE AREA AROUND HELSINKI

SUOMENLINNA

Suomenlinna is the modern name of a small group of islands on which the Swedes built a number of fortifications, bastions and small harbours in 1747. They called the place Sveaborg, i.e. "The Swedish Fort", and it was intended to serve as a protection for the Swedish empire against attacks by the Russians.

These islands were the scene of many battles, both during the Russo-Swedish conflict and during the Crimean War, when they were bombarded by the English. When Finland gained its independence in 1917, they took the name of Suomenlinna, which means "The Fortress of Finland".

In 1991, UNESCO included the fortified complex of Suomenlinna in its list of the World's Historical Heritage, a recognition of the important function it has played ever since the time of its construction. Suomenlinna is also a vast open-air museum, where it is possible to visit fortifications dating back to the second half of the nineteenth century – a series of Russian barracks built in wood, the villa, the **tomb of Commander Ehrensvärd**, and the **Museum** which bears his name, in which there are ancient furnishings and original maps and charts.

There are also other war museums, such as the **Museum of Coastal Defence** and the **Military Museum**, but museums devoted to the arts of peace are not forgotten; they include the **Armfelt** and the very famous **Centre of Nordic Art**. In addition, there is also a **Museum of Dolls and Toys**.

The Suomenlinna Islands are a favourite spot among the locals for passing a day strolling around and inspecting the bunkers which

The island-fortress of Suomenlinna, seen from above.

are dotted all over the territory, or enjoying a picnic in the country. Strangely enough, although they are so popular, the islands never give the impression of being over-crowded, except, that is, when one boards the ferry to return to the city.

ESPOO

This city is situated to the west of Helsinki, and built like a massive industrial suburb which lacks a real urban centre. Apart from its **Parish Church** in grey stone, dating from the second half of the fifteenth century, and a number of **Museums** such as the **Vintage Car Museum**, or the **Glims**, dedicated to folklore, and the **Clock Museum**, the most notable feature of Espoo is its possession of a number of examples of avant-garde architecture. This applies especially to Tapiola, a zone to the south of the city, and a pioneering example of urban planning, built in 1952 by some of the most innovative architects of that period – Aarne Ervi, Aulis Blomstedt, Vilyo Rewell, and Pentti Ahola. The architectural complex is built on several levels, and decorated with laminated surface materials; the elaborate geometrical structures of the buildings, and their extreme whiteness, blend harmoniously with natural elements such as water, or the green of the magnificent woodlands near which this complex has been deliberately situated. It includes a number of structures such as a swimming-pool, a covered market, a hotel, a church and a special school.

Another very interesting building is at **Otaniemi**, the University City of Espoo. This is where the world-famous **Polytechnic** is to be found; its central building, the **Auditorium Maximum**, was designed by Alvar Aalto. The building, in the form of an amphitheatre, is in a high position which follows the hilly contours of the surrounding countryside, and is visible from all parts of the campus. The fan-shape of this great hall responds

to a specific functional need: Aalto in fact always gave first priority to the question of lighting, and then to that of acoustics, and in this case he achieved excellent results by using a wide circular form made up of bricks, copper and glass.

The **Dipoli Student House** of the Polytechnic is also a fine building, by Reima and Raili Pietilä. The structure blends curved and geometrical forms organically, linking them to each other in rectangular orders. The result is a pleasing asymmetrical order, highlighted by the use of materials such as reinforced concrete, copper, wood and glass.

KIRKKONUMMI

Close to the small town of **Kirkkonummi**, near **Lake Hvitträsk**, are the houses of the architects Lindgren, Saarinen and Gesellius, dating from the beginning of this century. The three architects chose this place as their own "studio", and designed the buildings in their preferred style – the National-Romantic. The houses built with logs can be visited, including the interiors; they are decorated with great style and attention to detail. There is also a **Museum**, which houses several examples of vintage cars from the period of the building.

VANTAA

This is where Helsinki's Vantaa airport is situated. It is worth a visit for the famous **Heureka** Centre, the Museum of interactive science, where visitors – as well as exploring the many exhibition rooms – can also carry out experiments for themselves, and play an active role in understanding the mysteries of the most elaborate scientific discoveries. In the **Verne Theatre**, inside the Centre, it is possible to watch projections, programmes and multimedia shows which should definitely not be missed.

The Heureka Scientific Research Centre.

PORVOO

The city of **Porvoo** stands on the banks of the river of the same name, about fifty kilometres from the capital. It is one of the oldest cities in Finland; in the mediaeval period it was a flourishing trade centre, and the Swedish King Magnus Eriksson gave it its first charter in 1346.

Its romantic position on the banks of the river, its wooden houses, still in excellent state of preservation, and its narrow stone-paved streets have made it an ideal place for poetic inspiration. Many Finnish poets and artists such as Ville Vallgren, Albert Edelfelt, and Johannes Linnankoski in fact chose it as their ideal place of residence.

Johan Ludvig Runeberg, Finland's national poet, also fell under the spell of this peaceful spot; we can pay a visit to the house where he lived when he came to Porvoo, a well-preserved building, in the part of the city that looks out on the river, and has kept the original furnishings belonging to the great poet, whose remains lie in the old town cemetery. Right beside Runeberg's House, there is the **Runeberg Museum of Sculpture**, which houses the work of the poet's son, Walther Runeberg.

This is not the only Museum here: among many others we should mention the **Edelfelt-Vallgren Museum**, the **Yrjö A. Jäntii Art Collection** and the **Doll Museum**.

The city also has a fine mediaeval cathedral, which played an important role in the nation's history. The first Finnish Diet (Parliament) met there in 1809, after the Nation became an autonomous part of the Czarist Russian Empire.

The little town of Porvoo stands on the banks of the river of the same name.

Two views of Helsinki.

SOUTHERN FINLAND

This is the most populous area of the country, and also the richest in historical reminders such as churches, castles, and fortresses which bear witness to its cultural diversity.

It is also a large and wide-ranging tourist area, offering visitors a complete portrait of Finland, from its natural environment of forests, islands and thousands of lakes and rivers, to its historical cities and the huge variety of its cultural and sporting activities.

TURKU
THE FIRST CAPITAL
OF FINLAND

Turku occupies a unique place among the historical cities of Finland. It is the country's most ancient city, officially founded in 1229.

Standing at the mouth of the River Aura, Turku has close links with Sweden, and about ten percent of its population are Swedish-speaking. Its historical importance is witnessed by the presence of the mediaeval Cathedral and the Castle. Turku was, in fact, Finland's first capital, the seat of its bishop, and the city in which the first Finnish-speaking university was founded.

No visit to the city is complete without including the **Castle**, a grey stone building begun in the thirteenth century when Finland was subjected to administrative control by Sweden. The building grew constantly until it became a real fortress, made up of several towers and two blocks of buildings which rise to four floors.

Inside the castle, the city's **Historical Museum** has been established; the magnificent collection on display gives a detailed idea of the past of Turku and of the whole nation. In addition, concerts and Renaissance-style banquets are organized in the Castle.

The **Cathedral** of Turku is the city's oldest building, and is the national shrine of the Evangelical-Lutheran Church, in which some of the famous people who have contributed to the history of the nation are buried. It dates from 1287, and has been restored and extended several times. The style is Romanesque

The River Aura at Turku. Over the years, the banks of this river have become the home of many of the city's cultural institutions, such as the museum dedicated to Sibelius, the Library, and the Civic Theatre. It is also from here that the cruises around the nearby archipelago set out. Some boats moored at the riverside have been converted into typical local restaurants.

Turku: the Castle which has housed the city's historical Museum since 1881.

The Cathedral of Turku

and Gothic; the church has a high tower rebuilt by the architect Engel after the destructive fire of 1827. The interior has been expanded by a number of side-chapels, and consists of three wide naves.

Near the Cathedral is the **Monument to Mikael Agricola**, the Finnish sixteenth century reformer, disciple of Luther and Bishop of Turku. He is famous for his translation of the Bible into Finnish, and his work in developing the written Finnish language.

Many of the city's buildings were destroyed after the great fire of 1827, but the **Artisan Quarter (Luostarinmäen Käsityöläismuseo)**, on the little hill of Vartiovuori was completely saved from this because of its elevated position.

Its narrow streets and charming courtyards bear witness even today to the life and work of the artisans who lived here at the end of the eighteenth century. There are in fact artisan workshops and studios where work still goes on according to the techniques handed down from father to son, and there is a **Handicraft Museum** in some of the original eighteenth century wooden houses: here the craftsmen produce their creations, using the ancient implements handed down by their ancestors. During the summer, the area is alive with folk-dancing and popular concerts.

Something of interest can be found in every square in Turku: Cathedral Square has its university buildings and the **Sibelius Museum**, and is the cultural heart of the city, while the commercial centre, usually full of life, is in the **Kauppatori**, the Market Place, ringed by high-quality hotels and banks.

The **Qwensel House** is also worth a visit; it contains a **Museum of Pharmacy**, and nearby there is an excellent café.

There is no lack of parks in the town, and one of the most enjoyable visits is to the hundreds of delightful islands over which the city has extended in the course of time. With a little luck, the ferryboat ride from one island to another may be free.

It is also possible to reach the tourist town of **Naantali** by ferry. It is famous for its warm springs, and for its typical wooden houses gathered around the fifteenth century convent dedicated to St Brigid. It is here that the President of Finland has his summer residence, and this is certainly one of the most popular resorts among Finns for their holidays – especially the children. This is partly due to the fact that it was here in Naantali that the **Entertainment Park of the World of the Moomin** was initiated. The Moomin are popular characters created by the imagination of the writer Tove Janssen.

In the Turku district the National **Park of Saaristomeri** has been created: a veritable mosaic of rocky islands and outcrops covered with a rich and varied vegetation, where traces of the ancient inhabitants of the place can still be found.

The Entertainment Park of the Moomin – imaginary characters created by the writer Tove Janssen.

AN ISLAND FOR EVERYONE: THE ALAND ISLANDS

There are so many islands in the **Åland** archipelago (Ahvenanmaa in Finnish) that theoretically there could well be one for every visitor. The archipelago is in fact formed of around 6500 islands, islets and great rocks, which about ten thousand years ago began to emerge around the great rugged central island. Many of them are still intact and exactly as nature designed them.

The most imposing point among the islands is **Orrdalsklint**, in the Saltvik area, which reaches a height of about 420 feet. One can get to the top and from the wooden guard tower placed there admire a splendid view of the surrounding archipelago, where among other islands we can see Geta, Brandö, Föglö, Sund, Kökar, Sottunga, Saltvik, Vårdö and Finström.

In the valley between the hills of Saltvik, there is a rare **Stone Age village**, and a visit to this helps to understand the life of the primitive inhabitants of the Åland, when they lived in huts, used stone axes, and moved about from island to island in their canoes made of hollowed-out logs. This area has always been very fertile, as the numerous pre-historic finds, cemeteries and remains of ancient Viking forts make clear.

The islands are a real paradise for lovers of fishing: salmon, pike, sea-trout, salmon-trout, herrings, giant turbot and bass all abound in these unpolluted waters in great shoals, constantly repopulated to allow the conservation of fish resources.

Sailing enthusiasts too have a wonderful choice of outings in the Åland islands: the sea-routes are clearly indicated and the harbours provide a welcome with excellent services.

Sea and sailing have always been matters of life and communication for the archipelago, since they have been the most natural way of carrying on trade and keeping contact with the rest of the world. The islands have always attracted large numbers of mariners to them because of their strategic position, and for this reason they have often been the scene of important events in the country's history.

The capital of the archipelago is **Mariehamn**, a name deriving from Maria, the wife of Czar Alexander II, who gave orders for the town to be founded, in 1861. In the main street is the fascinating **Åland Museum**,

The artisans' quarter in Turku.

The Island of Brandö.

which illustrates the life and history of the islands right up to our own times. At the end of the street, near the town's western harbour, we find another excellent museum in the brig **Pommern**, actually set up inside the ship. It is dedicated to the golden age of sail, and is of great historical interest.

The seafaring tradition of the city is still eloquently evidenced by the schooner L*inden* and the ketch A*lbanus*, which are anchored in the eastern harbour of Mariehamn. For lovers of the sea and navigation, the **Maritime Museum of the Åland Islands** is of special interest. A sight which should not be missed, not far from the town, is

the island of **Eckerö**. This tourist spot is only two hours from Sweden, and the most westerly municipality of Finland. It has a splendid **Post Office**, built on the orders of Alexander II and designed by the architect Engel; its grandeur may take one somewhat by surprise, sited as it is in such a small village.

In another of the islands, **Sund,** a substantial number of the historical treasures of the archipelago are to be found. Among these is the ancient castle of **Kastelholm**, the origins of which are said to go back to the fourteenth century. It was a building of enormous strategic importance during the period of

Swedish rule; at the time of writing it is still in process of restoration. Far more recent are the ruins of the **Fortifications of Bomarsund**, a witness to the period of Russian domination in Finland. The main fortress, completed in the first half of the 19th century, was meant to hold a very large number of soldiers.

The whole complex of fortifications was bombarded during the Crimean War, and since it was badly damaged, it was never rebuilt.

In **Finström**, a very beautiful church in the typical local grey stone is dedicated to St Michael, and is one of the finest in the

Karlsgården Museum in the Sund District.

Old boat hung at the side of a wooden house in the Karlsgården Museum in the Sund District.

The Pommern, a museum-ship moored in the harbour of Mariehamn. It once served for the transport of grain between Australia and England.

whole archipelago, with its frescos and exquisite wood inlay decoration.

All this is to be found in the Åland Islands, but there is even more: they should be visited not just for their historical heritage or their museums. The most exhilarating experiences can be enjoyed by touring around by bicycle, or by coasting their shores in a small boat, in direct contact with a natural environment which is always varied and stunning. Long walks are also possible, along the paths which wind from the higher land, down through fields and woods, and eventually bring you to the shore. This is a world which it is impossible to describe; it needs to be experienced.

One of the many churches of the Åland Islands, at Eckerö.

In every church there is always a sail pinned to the ceiling. These are votive offerings from the fishermen, who since they had to remain at sea for a long time, prayed to God for protection.

Windmills in the Sund District.

THE COAST OF THE GULF OF FINLAND

The most southerly town of Finland is **Hanko**, situated in a particularly strategic position. For this reason, ever since it was founded in 1874, it has always had a considerable military importance, and its history is punctuated by battles and conquests. When Finland was part of Czarist Russia, the city was popular for its warm springs, and many well-off Russians built fine villas along the coast.

During the summer, the city of Hanko comes to new life for the **Hanko Regatta**, the most famous sailing event in the country, which takes place every year in the first weekend of July. On this occasion, the town fills with people and the atmosphere becomes cheerful and festive.

According to the Finns, the city of **Tammisaari** is the most beautiful of the southern coast; certainly its wooden architecture is in an excellent state of preservation.

The narrow streets of the old

A *fine house in Hanko*.

THE ELK

One of the most important of Finland's mammals is the elk. Despite the fact that for centuries it has been the sought-after prey of every hunter, there are still, even today, many elks present in the boundless stretches of woodland and forest of central-southern Finland.

This large mammal feeds on the youngest twigs of the birch, the willow and the aspen, but it often wanders into the newly-planted forest areas where it is easier to find the tenderest young shoots. Sometimes it is necessary to chase it away from the fields, because it loves to stop and graze on the young corn as soon as it begins to grow.

It often exceeds a horse in size, and in weight it may reach as much as half a ton.

The number of specimens to be found today in Finland is around 300,000, and recently there has been a trend towards an increase.

This means that each year, a hunt is authorised: for every hunting season, which begins on the last Saturday in September and lasts until 15th December, about 40,000 to 45,000 hunting licences are issued.

centre carry the names of the crafts which were carried on there, and the buildings facing on to these streets, all still inhabited, date from the sixteenth century; i.e. to the period when King Gustavus Wasa of Sweden promoted Tammisaari from a fishing village to a full-scale city. The majority of the people who live here are Swedish-speaking. Recently part of the archipelago surrounding the city has been declared a National Park. The **National Park of the Archipelago of Tammisaari** includes an area of the sea and part of the archipelago right in front of the city. There is also an ancient farm complex which has been restored, where information is available on the characteristics of the area. In the summer of 1995, the "Gnägget" Visitors' Centre was also opened.

Another of the ancient small towns on the shores of the Gulf of Finland is **Loviisa**, which dates from 1745, and takes its name from the Swedish Queen Lovisa Ulrika. The character of the town is influenced by the former military stables, a small but charming town museum, and a neo-Gothic church, one of the few built in this style in Finland. Here too we find narrow streets and picturesque cafés and restaurants. A sight not to be missed while you are in these parts is the island-fortress of **Svartholm**, an interesting testimony to the military history of the country.

The most important exporting port of the Gulf of Finland is unquestionably **Kotka**, also known as the City of the Seas. It could be said that the city forms a single unit with nearby **Karhula**, a more modern township. Kotka is the old city, and the greater part of it is spread out on a peninsula created at the mouths of two branches of the river Kymi.

Worth a visit is the **Orthodox Church of St Nicholas**, the oldest building to have survived the almost complete destruction of the city during the Crimean War. Kotka also has an interesting building which Czar Alexander III caused to be built in 1889: this is the **Little Imperial Fishing Lodge of Langinkoski,** which the Czar used to visit frequently, and where he and his family lived, by all accounts, in great simplicity, and without servants. It is even said that the (British) Czarina personally cooked the meals and that the Czar himself saw to the water supply and the logs for the fire!

The last important city before the border with Russia is Hamina, where the Treaty of the same name was signed. By this treaty, Sweden ceded Finland to Russia in 1809.

The city is rather unusually shaped, since its urban plan is circular; a great rarity in Finland. There are two main streets which form two concentric circles, the "Little Circle" (Pikkuympyrä), and the "Great Circle" (Isoympyrä). The walls surrounding the centre of the city were part of an eighteenth century complex of fortifications.

The town of Tammisaari in the autumn.

WESTERN FINLAND: SEA AND NATURE HAND IN HAND

Another important arrival-point in Finland for those coming from Denmark or Sweden, could be the western coast, a large region which is now undergoing considerable development as a tourist zone, while not losing its authentic character. The sun is rarely absent, and this, for a such a northern area, is a real blessing. The land is quite flat, and rich in thick woodlands, their greenery a joy to behold and to enjoy at first hand. The needs of every kind of visitor are catered for in this area: for lovers of the sea, for those who want to immerse themselves in the natural landscape and for those who prefer visiting towns and peaceful villages. On the subject of towns: on the coast above the Åland islands, we find the delightful town of **Uusikaupunkti**, founded in 1617, surrounded by a romantically beautiful archipelago of hundreds of islets. It is famous for its windmills, situated on **Myllymäki Hill**. There were once a dozen or so; now only four remain, and in one of them the **Folk Museum** is housed. The town still has many fine wooden houses in its nineteenth century quarter of the old centre, and there is a historic church dating from 1629.

Not far away is the seaside village of **Pyhämaa**, whose church, though not especially interesting on the outside, has a carefully preserved wooden interior, painted with intricate floral decorations and representations of the life of Jesus. This is the work of Christian Wilbrandt, and is dated 1667. As we head north along the coast, we find an important historical city, **Rauma**, famed for its quarter composed of wooden houses. There are in all about six hundred buildings, which make this the largest wooden-built quarter in Scandinavia. It is so well preserved that UNESCO recently decided to include it in its list of the World's Historical Heritage. Rauma also has many interesting museums, such as the **Marela House Museum**, the original dwelling of a shipbuilder

Pori.

of the nineteenth century, or the **Kirsti House Museum**, which displays the furnishings and hangings of a genuine sailor's house. There is also the **Rauma Art Museum**, and the fine Town Hall, the **Raatihuone**. Along the narrow streets of the wooden quarter there are many small shops and studios of local artists and craftsmen; a sight not to be missed. The town is also famous for its drum-lace work, and every year at the end of July the Week of Lace is celebrated here. In Rauma there is also a rarity for Finland: the **Church of the Holy Cross**, one of the most ancient in the country, dating back to the fifteenth century when it was part of a Franciscan monastery. Not far from the city is the island of **Reksaari**, a beautiful place to experience nature and the sea at first hand. It can be reached by ferry, and it is possible to stay overnight.

Near **Vammala**, heading inland, it is worth taking a walk of about two kilometres in an area protected by the WWF, to **Vehmaaniemi**, where one can follow a beautiful natural route winding along a peninsula. Apart from the natural beauties, some remains of a Stone Age settlement can be seen in this area, including some tombs. Travelling further along the coast, we come to the small town of **Pori**, a well-known Finnish cultural centre, famous above all for the annual International Jazz Festival which is held on the island of Kirjurinluoto. There are also long sandy beaches, equipped for

all kinds of water sports, at **Yyteri**. It stands on the new panoramic coast road linking Pori to Meri, and is the best place in Finland from which to observe migratory birds. At the far end of the peninsula of Pori, a sight not to miss is the picturesque fishing village on the island of **Reposaari**. Peacefully undisturbed, and linked to the land by a small bridge, it is a place to enjoy the best fish specialities. Further along the much-indented western coastline, we come to the little town of **Kristiinankaupunki**, another bilingual place like many of the towns facing across to Sweden. Here is yet another charming historic centre with fine wooden houses. One of the narrowest streets in the whole of Finland is here: the **Kissanpiiskaajankuja**, or in English, Catwhippers' Lane. It is less than three yards wide. Close to this town, on the island of **Kiili**, is a fine open-air museum, the **Museum of Kiili** which looks directly out to sea. Ancient buildings and objects of great historical importance to the area are on display. Right at the meeting point with the sea stands a small chapel built in wood. The most northerly city on this coast is a quiet, peaceful place. **Kaskö**, with its almost two thousand inhabitants, is the smallest city in Finland. The town stands on an island linked to the mainland by two bridges, and its old centre - consisting, it goes without saying, of wooden houses - is perfectly preserved.

Top: the city of Rauma.
Bottom: Kokkola, left, and Pietarsaari, right.

OSTROBOTHNIA

Many places of great interest from the point of view of culture, landscape and tourism are to be found in the region facing the Gulf of Bothnia, which penetrates deeply into the Scandinavian peninsula, carving out a great gulf between Sweden and Finland.

Among these, one of the most important is the city of **Vaasa**, founded in 1606, when it became the capital of Ostrobothnia. Rebuilt almost entirely after a great fire in the second half of the nineteenth century, it took on its present "imperial" appearance after the rebuilding, typified by elegant greystone buildings. The rebuilt city faces out to sea, and is in fact almost surrounded by it since it is completely built on small peninsulas and bays. The remains of the former city which was destroyed by the fire are to be found in the village of **Vanha-Vaasa.**

It is easier to understand the traditions and the cultural significance of Ostrobothnia after a visit to the **Museum of Ostrobothnia,** housed in a fine architectural complex by Eino Forsman, in the classical style of the 1920's. It has much evidence of the cultural and social history of the region, which consists of the part of Finland along the eastern shores of the Gulf of Bothnia. A part of the collection especially rich in objects and artistic worth is the *Hedman Collection,* which includes several Flemish and Italian works, worth a visit in themselves.

There are many other cities along the coast of the Gulf: the small town of **Uusikaarlepyy**, with its seventeenth century **Church** possessed of a very beautiful interior, and the **Water Tower** from which there is a wonderful view along the coast; or the city of **Pietarsaari**, with a very well-preserved historic centre, known as S*kata*, full of interesting 18th and 19th century buildings.

This is where the Finnish national poet, Runeberg, was born, and the

Setting sail.

city is scattered with reminders of him, including his old school, today a museum dedicated to his memory. Anchored in the harbour is the **Jacobstads Wapen,** a new vessel built according to seventeenth century designs.

Another of the Gulf coast cities is **Kokkola,** which seems fairly ordinary when viewed from outside, but contains a beautiful ancient "heart" with quiet streets and pretty, well-preserved buildings. There are several Museums, and islands like **Tankari** which repay a visit.

From the standpoint of landscape, the inner part of the region is in the geographical baricentre of Finland. This coincides more or less with the small town of **Oulainen,** where in October to November a lively music festival is held. The area is interesting above all because it is situated near the river Pyhäjoki, brimming with fish and very popular for salmon-fishing.

There are plenty of opportunities for sport and for the appreciation of nature in these parts. A very beautiful – and also adventurous – canoing route winds its way along an itinerary of about fifty kilometres, in the direction of Pohjanlahti. Furthermore, the whole area is covered with splendid forests, where wild mushrooms and forest fruit can be found. And if the call of the sea is strong once again, the sandbanks of Kalajoki are only half an hour away by car.

The only National Park in the region is at **Rokua**. This is the smallest and most original of the Finnish National Parks, and is the special favourite of those who love nordic flora, because it is covered with a very unusual species of white lichen.

Other areas of natural interest are **Lake Oulujärvi**, the fourth largest lake in the country, and the course

Oulu City Theatre.

of the river **Kiiminkijoki**, whose waters form part of a special international conservation programme.

Much further inland lies the hilly range of **Iso-Syöte**, near the village of Pudasjarvi. This is the southern-most range of Finland, 1400 feet high, and surrounded by thick protected forest. Long hikes are possible here, carefully marked out for walkers, and in winter the area is the centre of a skiing district. Another attractive city on the coast of the Gulf of Bothnia is **Oulu**, which was already a major centre for the trade in vegetable tar in the middle ages. It is an important university town, and in its research centre at **Tietomaa** scientific and technical phenomena are reproduced on the basis of everyday events. The islands which surround it offer plenty of interesting excursions: on one of them is the green park of **Ainolapuisto**, with its fine **Museum of Northern Ostrobothnia**. On the island of **Turkansaari,** on the other hand, an excellent open-air museum has been created. The remains of a seventeenth century fortress can be found at **Linnan-saari**, and a historical display has been laid out in one of its towers. Not far away is **Nallikari**, with its fine beach, its entertainment park, and a warm-springs centre.

The small town of **Kemi** is in the most northerly part of the Gulf, and its main attraction is the gigantic ice-breaker *Sampo*, which in winter sails along the greatest glacier in Europe, and can carry up to 150 passengers. The **Gallery of Precious Stones** should not be missed: apart from a priceless collection of rare gems, it also contains the famous *Crown of the King of Finland*, which – considering that the country has never had a king – is certainly a somewhat curious oddity!

The undergrowth of lichen in the National Park of Rokua.

WOODS AND FORESTS IN FINLAND

Nature is an integral part of the life of the Finns, who are accustomed from childhood to making good use of all the activities that can be carried on in contact with nature. It could hardly be otherwise, given the special character of the terrain, covered for the most part with woods, forests, lakes and waterways.

Forests, in particular, make up more than half the surface of the country. The majority of the territory in which they grow lies within the wider northern European zone extending from Russia to the most westerly part of Scandinavia. The vegetation consists above all of conifers such as the fir, the pine and the birch – the latter is unquestionably the dominant tree in the Finnish part of the territory. Its tall, pale, slim form and its leaves lightly stirred by the wind have inspired many traditional songs, which celebrate this tree and its leading role in the nordic landscape.

Other tall trees to be found in Finland include willow, alder, aspen, and mountain-ash, while in the more southerly area of the country, the oak is found in great abundance.

The typical lake and forest countryside of southern Finland.

The nation's patrimony of forest and woodland is vital to the national paper and woodcraft industries; it has always been a symbol of wealth and well-being for Finland, so it is natural that the work of conserving and replanting of the huge areas of forest should be a major concern for the country. Moreover, wood is still one of the raw materials for construction, both in housing and in handicrafts.

The exploitation of the forests is today the subject of constant control by the appropriate authorities, since both the bad atmospheric conditions and a diminished concentration of nutritives in the subsoil could well cause slower growth in the forests which will take the place of the present ones in the future. Great attention is therefore paid to environmental protection and to the problems of pollution, matters to which the whole population of Finland is highly sensitive.

CENTRAL AND EASTERN FINLAND

A kind of transitional area between the Lake District and Lapland, east-central Finland is huge in extent but very thinly populated. The landscape is still untouched – green and thickly wooded, with unpolluted lakes and rivers which leave a deep mark both on the countryside and on the memory. The view is sometimes what we can imagine an ancient Stone Age hunter might have enjoyed, and who knows what gods and goddess of nature may not still be hiding away in the valleys and canyons, on the shores of the north-eastern lakes, or wandering in the twilight in the majestic shades of the forest? They could certainly not have chosen a better place.

Rushing rivers and forests of firs and birches are typical of east-central Finland.

Much of Finnish territory is also covered with marshes.

THE SWEET SONG OF KARELIA

Northern Karelia is a specially significant region for Finland: being so close to Russia, and having suffered the consequences of the second world war, in which it lost the southern part of its territory, the Karelian Isthmus and the region of Salla, it can be considered in a way the symbol of national patriotic consciousness.

In addition, this land has for many years been the chosen guardian of the roots of Finnish culture: because of this, poets and painters have often taken it as a source of inspiration for their works.

This may be because its landscape is still primordial, covered with enormous virgin forest, the haunt of bears and lynxes. Or it may be because the Karelians who settled here to escape from the new boundaries of Russia continued to keep their unique traditions alive: their orthodox religion and their cultural affinity with nearby Russia, coupled with a deep-seated love for their own land.

Karelia, then, is a land of song, of happiness, legend, friendship, Orthodox churches and unforgettable landscapes. But naturally, there is much else beside....

The capital of Karelia, **Joensuu**, is the home of the Northern **Karelia Museum**, situated on an island in the River Pielisjoki. Its wooden **Orthodox Church**, dedicated to St Nicholas, possesses some icons painted in St Petersburg. The **City Hall** was designed by Eliel Saarinen, in his most classical Jugend style. Each summer, Joensuu hosts a very famous music festival, which is attended by thousands of visitors.

The city also possesses a **Garden of Tropical Butterflies**, the most northerly of its kind on earth.

Not far away from the city, near the little town of **Outokumpu**, is Lake **Sysmäjärvi**, a real paradise for nature-lovers and birdwatchers. From the 1950's, the lake suffered serious ecological damage from the presence of the nearby mines. Today, however, thanks to careful work of recovery and reclamation, it is an even more heart-warming to be able to enjoy the luxuriant vegetation once again, and to watch the big flocks of rare birds which choose to make their nests here. Experts have identified as many as 72 different species.

Views of Lake **Viinijärvi**, much bigger than the above-mentioned lake, can be enjoyed by following a specially-designed spectacular route, along which are Orthodox churches and beautiful lakeside houses hidden away in the green depths.

In the direction of **Heinävesi**,

One of the lakes of Northern Karelia.

travelling along one of the most beautiful of the lake routes made up of canals, islets and unexpected water recesses, we find the **Orthodox Monastery of Valamo**. Founded around eight hundred years ago, this monastery was once on an island in Lake Ladoga, in a piece of territory which is now in Russia. In 1940 it was transferred to the place where it now stands, together with a great part of its treasures, such as liturgical articles and icons; some objects and furnishings, however, are to be found in the Orthodox Church Museum at Kuopio. The monastery houses the largest orthodox library in existence, and is the home of the first workshop in the northern world to specialise in the conservation of icons.

The monastery's hostel offers visitors the possibility of staying overnight and eating in its restaurant. It is a very popular place for visitors, and for this reason those seeking peace and quiet may be a little disappointed, but in general, tourists are welcomed – to some extent because visitors are in fact the monastery's only resource.

One can reach the Monastery by way of the highest-altitude canal system in Finland, that of **Varistaipale**, which has a gradient of nearly fifty feet. During the journey, one can also reach the nearby and more tranquil **Convent of Lintula**, where wax candles for use in the Orthodox churches of Finland are produced.

A visit to **Ilomantsi, the most easterly village of Finland,** will be one way of discovering the customs and traditions of Karelia. Here there is the "**House of the History of Song**" – a Centre of Runic Singing, engaged in the conservation and popularisation of this important cultural tradition. The themes of the popular songs are always inspired by events and customs of the various families, and they often deal with the subjects which inspired the most famous national epic poem, the *Kalevala*.

On the hill of **Parppeinvaara** it is possible to see one of the most interesting and typical villages of Karelia. Several singers of the typical tunes of the area, accompanied by a local instrument, the *Kantele*, can still be found here.

The Monastery of Valamo.

The interior of the Orthodox monastery of Valamo.

The National Park of Petkeljärvi.

The Church of Ilomantsi.

There is also a fine Orthodox Church in Ilomantsi; the **Pyhän Elias kirkko**, a place full of evocative associations. During the summer, several typical Orthodox religious feasts are celebrated here (*Praasniekka*), characterised by processions and traditional singing.

Another splendid place, which inspired the majority of local painters, and even a world-famous artist like Sibelius, (who had his own piano brought here), is the upper region of **Koli**, The Hill of Koli is what remains of mountains which, thousands of years ago, reached a height of 19,000 – 21,000 feet. Its wonderfully rich vegetation and a stunning view for anyone who reaches its peak, high above Lake Pielisjärvi, are unforgettable. The

area has now become the small **Koli National Park**, combining all the characteristics of northern Karelia, with its pine and birch woods flanking the innumerable watercourses. This is surely one of Finland's most famous and spectacular attractions.

Nor is it the only park in the region; not far away is the **Patvinsuo National Park**, a natural area dedicated especially to the preservation of the enormous heritage of local fauna. It also includes Lake Suomunjärvi, famous for its beautiful sandy shores. A warning: bears and other large mammals are likely to appear at any moment from unexpected hideouts!

The other Karelian National Park, that of **Petkeljärvi**, should also be mentioned. This has a surface area

of about six square kilometres, covered with pine forest, small rocky crests and, of course, lakes and islets.

Another town of some importance is **Lieksa**, the local authority of which has the unique distinction of possessing at least a hundred kilometres of boundary with Russia. This town was once inhabited by the Sami, one of the peoples of Lapland, but the Karelians drove them further north, and settled in the city.

Lieksa stands on the shores of Lake Pielinen, and has one of the finest open-air museums of popular architecture in the whole of Finland, with a large number of typical buildings, all fully furnished.

There is also a Lutheran Church

THE EPIC OF KALEVALA

Until the nineteenth century, the numerous legends and popular traditions of Finland were passed down orally from one generation to another, and no-one had ever thought to record them in epic form.

At the beginning of the nineteenth century, a number of eminent literary figures, including J.V.Snellman, began the work of promoting a new national consciousness of Finnish language and culture, up to that time neglected from the literary point of view in favour of Swedish. As a result of this, the need began more and more to be felt of a significant reference point for the nation's literature and history.

Elias Lönnrot, a doctor who was an enthusiast for popular stories and legends, as well as poetry, obtained a grant in 1829 from the Finnish Literary Society, to undertake research on the poetry, legends and traditions of his nation. He went to Eastern Karelia, the area where the largest number of poems, runic narratives and family sagas were preserved, handed down by way of ballad-singers who recounted them during festivals, or around the hearth in peoples' homes. In this way, a huge treasury of traditions, proverbs, ballads and customs was collected, and he brought all these together in a single great historical and mythical poem, the Kalevala, taken from the name of a Karelian village.

Published for the first time in 1833, the national poem of Finland became, from then onward, one of the pillars of the nation's culture, and it has been translated into about forty languages.

designed by Raili and Reima Pietilä in Lieksa, a real masterpiece of modern architecture.

In the area surrounding the town, there is **Vuonislahti**, where the sculptress Eeva Ryynänen has her studio. Her works are splendid sculptures in wood, in a highly original style, and they can be seen by visiting her studio which is open to the public. This artist has also built a wooden church in this area. The whole area is greatly recommended for fishing and canoing; there are many routes to try out, though always under instruction from the local experts. It is from here that the famous Bear Track begins, the **Karhunpolku**, an interesting planned itinerary winding northwards for 120 kilometres and passing through the Patvinsuo Park.

At **Nurmes** the birch-trees abound; its tree-lined avenues have great charm and the whole surrounding area is covered with thousands of these splendid trees.

In the town, a farm complex has been rebuilt, faithfully reproducing the features of another farm which fell inside the boundaries of Russian Karelia. This is the **Bomba House**, named after its builder, Jegor Bombin. This series of buildings witnesses to the kind of life of a big peasant family, and at the same time it preserves some of the customs and traditions of Karelia. Today it includes a restaurant, a tourist village and an open-air theatre, together with a tiny *tsasouna*, the typical Orthodox chapel.

Koli Hill.

Winter in Koli.

Countryside in the Nurmes area.

Lieksa: the floating of the timber.

The town of Nurmes at sunset.

Northern Karelia.

The Bomba House - Nurmes

TRAILING THE BEARS: FROM KUHMO TO KUUSAMO

In this part of Finland, the wildest and most untouched natural areas are to be found, where natural abundance is about to give way to the power of the great icecap. Here we find the magnificent lake landscapes and the first of the bare, barren hills that we shall meet with more frequently in Lapland, and here we can feast our eyes on landscapes of dramatically intense colours. It is possible to leave one's cares behind in a moving encounter with nature in the midst of deep forests or along the banks of rushing streams and rivers.

Moving northward, in the region of Kainuu, the visitor will be constantly reminded of the barren and savage surrounding landscape, and the tiny isolated villages set in it. A circular route has been created, the **Korpikylien tie**, which leads to all the most forgotten villages of the area, beginning with **Saramo** and travelling on to **Suomussalmi**, an important battleground during the second world war, when the Russians sought to conquer this zone.

A good departure point for visits to the area is **Kuhmo**, with its fine **Kalevalakylä Park**, dedicated to the era of Kalevala. And we should not overlook the little town of **Kajaani**, crossed by the river of the same name. Many people sit along the shores of the river to fish for salmon, e.g. near the seventeenth century **Castle**. From the town, the largest in Finland in terms of territory, with its 5458 square kilometres, many natural tracks spread out, all carefully signposted, and full of information about the surrounding beauty spots.

One of these is the **Waterfall of Hepoköngäs**, which with a drop of about 75 feet is the highest in the country. It lies between **Puolanka** and **Hyrynsalmi**.

In the region of **Kuusamo**,

National Park of Oulanka.

The rapids on the river Oulanka in the National Park which carries its name, in the Kuusamo area.

The waterfall of Hepoköngäs.

contrasting features are merged: on the one hand the plateau which forms it is covered with thick pine forests and dotted with hundreds of lakes and watercourses; on the other hand its closeness to the Arctic Circle renders it very similar to barren Lapland, which is only a very short distance away. If we add to this a scene from nearby Karelia, with its traditions and typical dwellings, we have a complete image of the manysidedness of this exceptional region.

The main attractions of this area are all connected with nature and the activities associated with it. In the local authority of Suomussalmi, for example, there is one of the most attractive excursion areas of the whole of eastern Finland at **Hossa**, where long narrow streams pour into huge, crystal-clear lakes. Fishing is one of the most satisfying activities in this zone, but it is

an unforgettable experience just to wander round the signposted routes, over 90 kilometres of them in all.

This area too has its National Park, **Oulanka**, where the most important waterways and natural features are concentrated.

The park is dotted with magnificent rapids such as **Taivalköngäs** and **Kiutaköngäs**, and there are others near the village of **Juuma**, the famous rapids of **Niskakoski**, **Myllykoski** and **Jyrävä**.

The best-known trekking route is called **Karhunkierros**, (the Bear Circuit) which passes through gorges, rapids, mountains and timeless forests, and touches most areas of the park, arriving eventually at **Rukatunturi**, a range from which on the clearest days one can see right across to Russia. Being so near to the foaming streams of Oulanjoki and Kitkajoki,

it will be hard to resist the appeal of the famous trout of Kuusamo. So don't forget to bring the fishing rod...

The park has the most varied flora; species typical of the South, East and North are all to be found there, living together in incredible profusion in this delicate ecosystem. The fauna is equally plentiful: bears, wolves, wolverenes, and the rarest species of oriental birds never seen elsewhere in Europe all live undisturbed here. In order to give some idea of the unique flora and fauna of this area, a special permanent exhibition has been arranged in the heart of the park itself.

Another of the wonderful attractions of the area to the south of Kuusamo is Lake **Julma Ölkky**, situated in a deep rocky gorge whose steep walls are sometimes more than 150 feet high.

The river Kitkajoki, along the Bear Path.

Sunset on the river Kitkajoki.

CENTRAL FINLAND AND THE LAKE DISTRICT

The most inland part of Finland is covered with hundreds of lakes and waterways, and interesting towns and forgotten villages are interspersed with magnificent forests. This is surely the way that we have all pictured this country at one time or another.

Aerial view of the town of Hämeenlinna.

LIVING ON THE WATER: THE WESTERN LAKE DISTRICT

This region includes some of the largest lakes in Finland, a number of parks which have been formed in countryside with wild and unspoilt landscapes, rivers abounding in rapids, and towns which are rich in historic and cultural associations.

We begin with the city of **Hämeenlinna**, famous for its thick woods, its glass-making and its fine **Aulanko Park** which possesses many exotic trees, pretty little houses and swans gliding along near the lake shores. There is also a small observatory in the park. The area has signs of habitation dating back to the ninth century, while the red brick **Fortress** which stands here was built by the Swedes in the thirteenth century, and now houses a **Folk Museum**.

It was here that one of the most famous of all Finland's personalities, the composer Jean Sibelius, was born. This has meant that the town has enjoyed a particularly flourishing musical development, often hosting a series of initiatives in that field. Sibelius' birthplace is now a **Museum** dedicated to his memory. Still in Hämeenlinna it is well worth visiting the **Prison Museum**, in the old prison of Häme, and the **Artillery Museum**, which houses a unique collection related to war history.

The other major town in this area is **Tampere**, reachable from Hämeenlinna by a ferry which follows a beautiful tourist route. The town is one of the most industrialised in the country, but it has nevertheless kept its human dimension. Initially built on an isthmus between two big lakes, it is now the biggest inland city in the whole of Scandinavia. Despite its strong industrial character the town has made good use of the natural features on which it has been built. The visitor need only climb the very high **Näsinneula Panoramic Tower** in the Särkäniemi Entertainment Park to obtain some idea of these natural surroundings. The city has numerous parks and leafy avenues.

On a small rise stands the **Lutheran Cathedral**, which has an unusual red steeply pitched roof, providing a pleasing contrast with the grey stone of the building. The heart of the city is in multi-coloured **Keskustori**, the market place, surrounded by important buildings such as the **Town Hall** in neo-Romantic style, the **Old Church**, dating from 1824, and the **Theatre**, a 1913 building. Among the many museums, we should

A night view of the town of Tampere.

mention the "**Sara Hildén**" Museum of Modern Art. In Tampere, there is the beautiful quarter known as **Pispala**, from where one can see the lakes which surround the city, or visit the old industrial installation in red brick, **Verkaranta**, which has now been rebuilt and adapted for use as handicraft workshops and boutiques. The Museum quarter of **Amuri** is also interesting; here the old wooden houses of the workers have been preserved, as well as its former shops and saunas. Tampere is famous for devoting much attention to artistic activity: theatre performances have been especially fostered, and every year the **Summer Theatre Festival**, very popular among the Finns, takes place in the city.

Tampere - The Metso Library, designed by the architects Raili and Reima Pietilä. Seen from above, it has the shape of a wild bird.

THE NATIONALPARKS

The **Isojärvi and Helvetinjärvi** National Parks are the two precious jewels set in the rich natural vegetation of this region. The first lies around the shores of Lake Isojärvi, surrounded by wooded hills, and many other lakes and tiny pools. Many good natural hikes are suggested, and it is possible to camp overnight in the park.

The second park, **Helvetinjärvi,** is near to what was once described as the prettiest village in Finland, **Ruovesi.** The main attraction of the park is its narrow gorge, which is the result of constant attrition by the ice, begun not less than then thousand years ago. Here too there are plenty of signposted routes, and overnight stays are possible.

The National Park of Isojärvi. The Open-air Museum.

The National Park of Helvetinjärvi.

THE CALL OF THE FOREST IN THE CENTRAL LAKE DISTRICT

The romantically beautiful territory which forms part of the centre of the country is occupied by the District of **Jyväskylä** and its surrounding area. The main feature of the whole district is the presence of thick, luxuriant forests, enormous lakes and fairly high peaks which enable one to take in the splendid surrounding view. All types of water-sports can be enjoyed in this area, but one of the great pleasures is to discover its charms by bicycle, or during long walks, which are perhaps the best way of meeting up with these generous and fascinating natural surroundings. The area is not densely populated, but the little towns and villages are always very lively with constant festivals and events. The city which gives its name to the district, **Jyväskylä**, is an important cultural and commercial centre as well as a tourist spot. There are numerous museums to visit, including the one dedicated to Alvar Aalto, who began his career as a designer and architect in this city and region. At least thirty buildings, all designed by him, provide unmistakable evidence of the growth in style and structure of this great artist. The district also possesses some of the best lakelands in Finland, the most beautiful of all being **Päijänne**. On one of its peninsulas is **Savutuvan Apaja**, where a number of ancient rural buildings typical of central Finland have been brought together. The place was awarded a prize in 1991 as the best tourist attraction in Finland, because of the accuracy of its historical and ethographical reconstructions. The haybarn carved out of the rock now houses a restaurant in which some of the tastiest local dishes can be sampled. On the shores of the lake, at **Muurame**, those who appreciate typically Finnish traditions, and who have at least once in their lives enjoyed the benefits of a sauna, will find the only open-air museum in the whole of Finland in which a large number of saunas from different periods are on display. The Museum is known as **Saunakylä** (the Sauna Village), and some of the saunas it possesses date from the eighteenth and nineteenth centuries, and are still in perfect working order.

In central Finland, as in the other

Jyväskylä.

Lake Päijänne.

The ski jumps at Lahti, a major winter sports centre.

THE MAGIC EFFECTS OF THE SAUNA

The sauna is a Finnish invention, and taking a sauna is a hygienic practice known to the inhabitants of this nordic land thousands of years ago. Even today, once or twice a week, and preferably on Saturdays, every Finn prepares to make use of this kind of benificent ritual, which has such incomparable effects.

It is the ideal place for bodily and mental purification; almost a sanctuary in which to recover one's physical and spiritual strength, allowing fatigue, stress and exhaustion to evaporate in the all-embracing, refreshing warmth.

The sauna, in which the ideal temperature is between 80 and 100 degrees Centigrade, may be a small cabin annexed to one's own apartment in the city, a public sauna with a swimming pool, or a small house near one's cottage beside the lake. The latter is unquestionably the best place for an effective, stimulating sauna: the lake in which to take a plunge afterwards is a few paces away; the birch twigs to stimulate circulation are just behind the house, and the wood for stoking up the fire, perfumed with resin, is there to produce the right kind of steam. The traditional sauna, or *savusauna*, ("Smoke-sauna") is still heated with wood, though electric ones are found, especially in the towns and the hotels. At the moment, there are about one million six hundred thousand saunas in Finland, for a population of around five million people.

"Vasta" - the birch twigs which are used to beat the body during the Sauna as a means of activating the circulation.

After-Sauna slippers made of birch-bark.

areas, there are vast numbers of routes to follow in search of close contact with nature, and they are very carefully organized and planned.

Along the miles of pathway belonging to these circuits, panels are posted explaining the special character of the local flora and fauna, and there are also some brief comments on the characteristics of the surrounding landscape. Among the many beautiful tracks to follow in this area, we might mention those which lead from **Kuusaa** to **Peurunka**, or the **Laajavuori** and **Muuramenharju** routes.

The variety and abundance of the many waterways make it possible to attempt canoing, including rapid-shooting, on the rivers. At the moment, the **Kuusaankoski** Rapids are among the favourites of those who like adventurous descents, but those which are found near the town of **Saarijärvi** can also provide canoists with a thrill of excitement.

The less sportingly-inclined may decide instead to take to the waters of **Lake Päijänne**, and take part in some of the many lake cruises which are organised: these make it possible to discover the beautiful **Keitele – Päijänne Canal**, which wanders along a route of about forty kilometres, and is broken up by five locks, with a change in level of around 70 feet.

Further to the south there are other important towns such as **Mikkeli**, an ancient city inhabited since the fourteenth century, or **Lahti** which is the southern entry port to the Lake District, and stands on the southern shores of Lake Päijänne.

The Lake District.

In the National Parks the oldest tree-trunks take on the strangest shapes. When they fall and rot in the undergrowth they contribute towards the nutrition of tomorrow's forest.

THE NATURAL AND CULTURAL ATTRACTIONS OF THE EASTERN LAKE DISTRICT

Undoubtedly the most important features of this area of southern Finland are again the hundreds of lakes which follow closely, one after the other, interspersed with thick, green and scented woods.

In the area of Savo, there are two great national Parks: **Linnansaari** and **Kolovesi**. The **Linnansaari National Park** lies within the local authorities of Savonlinna and Rantasalmi, and contains, in the lake complex of **Saimaa**, about twenty tiny islands with very varie-

THE SEALS OF SAIMAA

In the Saimaa Lake district lives one of the rarest animals still existing in the world. Its Latin name is Phoca hispida saimensis, but it is better known as the Freshwater Seal of Saimaa. The marble-style patterns of its beautiful pelt have also inspired the other name by which it is known – the "Marble Seal". The World Wildlife Fund has declared it a protected species, since barely a hundred specimens have survived, living exclusively in this area.

The history of this mammal goes back tens of thousands of years, when it lived among the glaciers. When the melting of the ice-cap submerged the surrounding land, great freshwater lakes were formed. And it was among these lakes that the seal remained a prisoner, unable to reach its marine habitat.

In order to survive, the seal was forced to adapt to a freshwater environment which was not its own normal one, and today it is one of the most interesting examples of adaptive capacity in the whole animal kingdom.

gated landscape and covered with pine and broadleaf forests. This is the habitat of one of the animals declared a protected species by the WWF: the *Saimaa Seal*, whose presence in these parts dates back to the ice-age.

Many rare birds also choose the islands of this lake to nest, and it is a delightful experience to observe them in their natural surroundings. The **Kolovesi National Park** has a smaller surface area than the preceding one, but is of equal interest. Here water dominates the scene completely, and the view is characterised by irregular steep rocks, carved out by the waters of the narrow canals which divide the islands, and which spread through this whole fascinating area with its ancient pinewoods, their outline shaped by the dark shapes of the red pines, and surrounded by rocky

peaks. Among the most interesting and evocative places for a visit in this area is **Punkaharju** with its long straight isthmus jutting out into the lake; one of the most important evidences of the glacial era, during which it was formed as a consequence of the great shifts in the glaciers. The view from the old panoramic route which runs along it is incomparable.

Not far from here is one of the greatest cultural centres in the country – **Retretti**, a strange construction in the cliffs, with extraordinary sound and light effects. In this artistic centre there are constant exhibitions, and wonderful concerts are held in the underground concert-hall, its acoustics unique in the world.

At **Lusto**, in the Punkaharju district, an interesting **National Museum** has recently been opened, dedicated

to the forests, and in the Punkaharju Park, one can find a variety of species of trees, some of them more than two hundred years old, such as the family of conifers made up of about forty examples. Among the many lakes, it is worth paying a visit to **Siikalahti** near Parikkala, to hear the singing of the innumerable birds as they make their nests and rest on their migratory journeys. Some rare species have chosen this for their nesting-place and it is especially noted for its nightbirds, such as the nightingales. Many tracks are laid out for visitors, all of them carefully signposted: it is an excellent way of exploring the natural and so far unspoilt habitat of these birds.

Here too there are plenty of occasions for delightful canoing excursions, including the **Oravareitti** route, in the area between Juva and Sulkava, which runs among rapids, lakes and rivers for more than fifty kilometres. There are also many excursions from **Enonkoski** and **Simanala**.

The main city of this area is **Savonlinna**, with its splendid **Castle of Olavinlinna**, dating from 1475, an imposing building flanked by massive towers. The castle is the superb setting for one of the most famous of Finland's summer events: the **Savonlinna Opera Festival**, held in July and August of each year.

Also in the vicinity of Savonlinna is the Wooden Villa of **Rauhalinna**, dating from 1900. This can be reached by boat from the city harbour; its romantic atmosphere makes it one of the favourite haunts of visitors, who can also enjoy a good meal in its excellent restaurant.

The Retretti Cultural Centre. This is an unusual museum carved out of the rock. It houses temporary exhibitions by international artists. Because of its exceptional acoustics, many concerts are performed here.

The cities of Lappeenranta (above) and Imatra are both important centres of southern
Karelia on the shores of Lake Saimaa. Lappeenranta is a premier summer vacation spot;
Imatra is best known for the Imatronski Rapids, which have been attracting tourists for
hundreds of years.
Bottom: one lake in the lake network of Saimaa.

Near the city, it is worth paying a visit to the largest wooden church in the world, which is to be found in **Kerimäki**, a small town of about seven thousand inhabitants. The reason why such a huge church is to be found in such a small place is easy to discover: it is said that the architect gave the carpenters the measurements in feet, but they then executed them in metres! The result that emerged is this gigantic construction, which can hold up to 3300 people.

Further north, in wonderful lakeland scenery, we come across another important town, **Kuopio**. The best point to take it all in in one glance is from the panoramic tower of **Puijo**, on the hill of the same name. From there you can see the splendid view of Lake **Kallavesi**, dotted with countless wooded islets.

Among the many museums to be seen in the city is the **Museum of the Orthodox Church**, which has some magnificent icons on display, and other sacred objects which were once in the area that has now become part of Russia.

The **Market Place** of the town is one of the most animated and colourful of all: as you wander round the stalls, the friendliness and good humour of the people strikes you immediately.

Among the most famous cultural events at Kuopio is the **Festival of Music and Ballet**, which is held at the beginning of every summer, and which welcomes thousands of visitors every year.

The Church of Kerimäki.

Lusto: The National Museum of the Forests.

The castle of Olavinlinna at Savonlinna.

Aerial view of the town of Savonlinna and Kuopio.

LAPLAND

The Arctic Circle, with all the thousands of associations which the name evokes, even among those who have never set foot there, is the southernmost part of Lapland. This means that this region of Finland has every claim to represent the myth of the "Far Frozen North", as popular with tourists as those of the Orient or Africa.

Here, visitors come to admire the extraordinary shades of the midnight sun in the summer, or in winter to peer out from the protective warmth of a *sami* tent in the midst of the snow at the rarefied light of the *kaamos*, the characteristic polar night illuminated from time to time by the brush-strokes of the breathtaking Aurora Borealis.

Lapland is a frontier region. One gets the feel of this immediately on arrival at **Enontekiö**, the little airport in the north-western part of the region. It is a little white and blue building in the middle of nowhere, where the birch and pine woods have already given way some distance back to soft rounded hills, *tunturi* covered with lichen and musk, the last representatives of a flora which will have soon to give way to the ice and freezing ferocity of a winter which may last as long as nine months.

The landscape of Lapland is not in fact made up of snow-covered peaks, or imposing glaciers or dizzy heights; on the contrary, it is all laid out on the horizontal plan, stretching out over the interminable reaches of the typi-

cal Arctic tundra, where only here and there some daring birch tree manages to assert itself. It is only interrupted by rivers or lakes, frozen over in the winter.

The highest peaks only reach just over 3000 feet, and are mainly found in the areas bordering Sweden and Norway. The highest is **Haltiatunturi (4300 feet)**, followed by **Saanatunturi (3350 feet)**.

In such an environment, which seems to many to be hostile and difficult, the reindeer is the undisputed ruler. Almost two hundred thousand of them live in this land, and they provide an inexhaustible source of sustenance for the inhabitants, who number about the same.

Almost everything belonging to the

Sami tent at Hetta.

Reindeer at Torassieppi.

reindeer is used – from the pelt to the antlers to the meat – a visit to **Torassieppi** is enough to make this clear. Here we can learn about the moments of greatest significance in the life of the herd – the birth of the young, the branding, the separation and the slaughter, but also by reflection the life that is lived by this unique people, the Lapps.

A section of this people belongs more properly to the ethnic group of the Sami, a Nordic population characterised by their colourful clothes of blue cloth, decorated in red and yellow; they also wear strange breeches with stitching made out of reindeer kin, and a tall hat decorated with coloured ribbons.

The Nordic Sami population consists of around seventy thousand people, of whom about 6500 live in Finnish Lapland. They occupy the territory divided up between Norway, Sweden, Russia and Finland. Almost all of them are united by their common language, *Same*, divided up into several dialects, and by a culture and tradition which are both unique in the world.

SKI RESORTS

Almost nowhere in the world are the conditions for skiing so favourable as they are in Finland. The very long skiing season in northern Finland begins in October and lasts at least until the middle of May. Almost all the winter sports centres have floodlit cross-country tracks and downhill slopes to extend the day's skiing. Apart from the numerous cross-country tracks and downhill slopes, Finnish ski resorts also provide a vast range of other winter activities, including snow boarding, snowmobile safaris, and dog- or reindeer-pulled sleigh rides. Moreover, Finnish ski schools are well-know and highly thought of at international level. One of the most popular and famous ski resorts in Lapland is Ylläs, the largest skiing centre in the Arctic icecap.

The cross-country tracks which branch out from here lead to other important winter sports centres, such as Levi, Muonio and Hetta, or cross the lonely landscape of Western Lapland, creating a network of tracks which extends for almost 1000 km.

Saariselkä, on the edge of the UKK National Park, is one of the best-loved winter sports centres in Finland, also ideal as a departure Joint for ski trips lasting several days.

Pyhä, close to the Pyhätunturi National Park, in the favourite destination of expert skiers. From here it is possible to visit the park on skis and ski the famous track which links "tunturi Pyhä" and Luosto.

Reindeer at Saariselkä.
Winter sports.

Sunset at Levi, Lapland.

WELCOME TO LAPLAND: ROVANIEMI

Rovaniemi is the capital and the access port to Finnish Lapland. It is a small town on the river Ounasjoki, and is quite modern, since it was rebuilt, after being destroyed by the German troops in the second World War, on the basis of a town-planning scheme by Alvar Aalto.

In the town, the **Lutheran Church** is worth a visit; it has an unsual fresco in the interior of the apse, showing Christ surrounded with Lapp people, with the whole scene portrayed in a typical nordic setting.

The architectural complex which Aalto also designed for the Municipal Theatre and the City Congress Centre is very fine.

Known as the **Lappia talo**, this was built in 1975. A Library is attached to it,

The Arktikum Museum and, in the background, the town of Rovaniemi. The interior of the Museum.

with a collection of 500,000 volumes, the most ancient of which dates back to 1561 and is written in Italian. The **City Hall** is also part of the complex designed by Aalto. Another of the town's attractions is the unusual **Arktikum Centre**, inaugurated in 1992. This is a long glass tunnel facing northwards, which delves into the depths of the earth, almost as if to signify the profound links of this people with nature. The **Lapland Museum** which is housed here is the best way to satisfy the visitor's curiosity about this land and its people; in 1994 it was awarded a prize as the best Museum in Europe. The Arktikum Centre also houses an institute involved in research into the people and the nature of the Arctic zones, and the results of this research are presented to the public in permanent exhibits and in the various short-term exhibitions held in the Centre. Near Rovaniemi is the demarcation line of the Arctic Circle (*Napapiri*) the imaginary line which in Finland marks the southernmost point at which the midnightsun can be observed. Santa Claus has his headquarters here, in the **Village of Father Christmas**, with its post office to which every year thousands of children address their Christmas requests. Santa Claus responds to each of them (supposed that he has got clear and readable addresses), sending personalised letters with his own special stamp.

Situated in the province of Rovaniemi, excavated in the depths of the *Syväsenvaara hill*, it's the **Santapark**, where you can enjoy the atmosphere of Christmas all year round. Together with Father Christmas, his elves and reindeer, this park offers a unique and unforgettable experience.

Dear Santa ...

Finland is the birthplace of Santa Claus, also known as Father Christmas. But have you ever wondered how old that generous old fellow dressed in red and sporting those white whiskers must be? According to some rumours, he's getting on for 500 years old, and he spends the best part of the year in the heart of Finnish Lapland, at Korvatunturi, where his innumerable helpers, the elves, make it possible for him to deal with the thousands of requests for presents which arrive, full of expectation, from all over the world. Korvatunturi, in the district of Savukoski, has about 2000 inhabitants and about 20,000 reindeer, apart from those belonging to Santa, of course.

As it is rather an out-of-the-way place, Santa Claus also has a workshop, with a lot of sleighs and reindeer, and his own personal post office near Rovaniemi, exactly where the Arctic Circle lies.

In his period of greatest activity - Christmas Eve - Santa Claus goes off with his sack overflowing with presents to almost every house in Finland; he knocks at the door, and asks how the children of the house have been behaving ... generally the children win his heart by singing a special little song, and finally the much-awaited present is delivered without further delay.

You want to know his address? Here it is:
Santa Claus
Arctic Polar Circle
96930 Rovaniemi, Finland

THE FINNS AND THE MYTH OF NATURE: LAPLAND'S NATIONAL PARKS

Finland's National Parks are protected areas in which nature has been left untouched, as far as possible, and one can enjoy it to the full as long as one shows equal respect for it, by following the rules of behaviour which safeguard it. This is the only way we shall be able to know and understand the deep sentiments of love, respect and gratitude which the Finns have for nature, an inexhaustible source of joy and serenity.

In the southernmost part of Lapland, near Kemijärvi, one of the four great national parks of this region has been created: **the National Park of Pyhätunturi**, which includes part of the Finnish mountain chain culminating in the peaks known as *Pyhä* and *Luosto*. It is characterised by steep cliffs, profound gorges and rocky surfaces. In the park there is a vistors'-centre, and many trekking paths are indicated. One of the most attractive routes is the deep gorge of Pyhäkuru, which cuts between the two peaks of Kultakero and Ukonhattu.

The **Urho Kekkonen National Park**, dedicated to the President of Finland who consolidated Finland's position on the international scene, extends for about 2550 square kilometres in the area from Saariselkä (it is also known by this name) to the huge forests where the river Nuorttijoki flows, to the east. Given the huge extent of the territory included in the park, it is possible to find every kind of flora and fauna there, making it a truly unique site. It is possible to stay overnight in some of the refuges, and the Information Centre for the park is to be found in **Tankavaara**.

In the latter village, situated near the park, many people are seized with gold fever in the summer

The National Park of Pyhätunturi.

The Urho Kekkonen National Park.

Lapland summer landscape.

season. By paying an entry-ticket to the gold-seeking area, it is possible to have a try at sifting a little gold from the river sand. All you need is a handy receptacle, a lot of patience, and a certain amount of luck! Every year there is a gold-diggers' competition, and the winner is named champion of the craft.

In the village the **Golden World** exhibition was opened in June 1995. The story of the discovery of gold in more than 20 countries of the world is on display here.

The largest park in Lapland, and indeed in the whole of Finland, is the **Lemmenjoki** Park, with its 2855 square kilometres of wild sub-Arctic conifer and birch forest, its bare rounded hills, rivers and marshes. The main attraction is the valley of the river which gives its name to the Park. Here too it is possible to make use of a Visitors' Centre to get to know more about the features of the place and to find out the best camping-sites.

The other park in Lapland is the **Pallas-Ounastunturi Park**, situated on a chain of hills at the foot of which the vegetation is the typical conifer forest surrounded by peat. Here too there is a very well-equipped Visitors' Centre, and you can camp or spend the night at places indicated by the Park Management.

As we head north we find many other small towns, and beauty spots along the wide roads which cut through this distinctive nordic countryside, characterised by low mountains (**tunturi**), clear streams, unusual vegetation and a few sizeable lakes in the most northerly area. In the south-east of Lapland there are lakes, like Kemijärvi, which abound in fish, and there are fast-flowing rivers which converge in this part of the region, forming thirty rapids. This makes it an ideal spot for those who enjoy rafting.

THE CENTRE OF LAPP CULTURE AND TRADITION

At the end of March, at **Hetta** in the north-west of Lapland, there is the annual *Feast of Mary*, the most important event in which the Sami community takes part. For two days, the little town, no more than a few houses scattered around a chapel, is enlivened by stalls, handicrafts, hats, gloves, boots made from suede or leather, axes, lassoos for the reindeer, and so on. The fair is attended by the Sami, who come to the town to take part in the competitions which are held there; for the occasion they wear their bright traditional blue and red costume.

The key event of the festival is the traditional reindeer race, but above all the reindeer-catching rodeo, using lassoos – a real test of skill among the breeders. At the moment there are 42 communities herding reindeer, which represent the principal resource of Lapland, apart from tourism. There are two special occasions each year in which the reindeer are rounded up by the breeders: the first in the period of the feast of St John, for the "branding", a marking operation which is still done by hand, and involves the incision in the animal's ear of a special mark which is the "brand". In Finland alone around 16,000 different marks are used, so that a breeder can recognise his own deer from others' at a single glance. The second rounding-up occasion is in November, for the slaughter; generally, the older females and the males of more than a year old are eliminated.

The *Sami* language is made up of three dialects of Ugro-Finnish origin. In order to preserve and promote the Sami language and

Sami costumes.

Huskies.

Reindeer race.

THE REINDEER

There are very many reindeer in Finland. The herds of this placid mammal prefer the tundra of Lapland, where they find plenty of lichen, though when necesary they will also eat mushrooms and birch and willow shoots.

The reindeer herds live in the wild state, but they are herded into large, specially built corrals twice a year by the Lapp herdsmen, for the operation of "branding" of the young, and for slaughter. The reindeer is the principal source of sustenance, apart from tourism, for these people: since they are so valuable, every breeder recognises "his own" deer on sight, simply by looking at their ears. All the deer of a herd have a recognition mark, which consists of an incision in the ear. Each individual breeder or cooperative of breeders has his or its own typical mark, and is capable of recognising it from among a total of 16000 others.

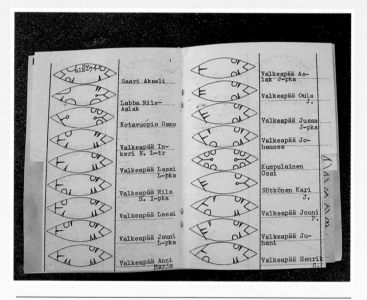

The register of the Sami Cooperative, with the symbols of the owners' marks, incised in the ears of the reindeer.

In November the deer are again herded in by the breeders for slaughter: in general, it is the males that have reached more than one year old, and the oldest females, who are slaughtered for meat and pelts.

In order to find food in the winter, the reindeer move down to the great conifer forests south of Lapland, where the layer of snow covering the plants on which they feed is thinner. But in the summer they return northward, and settle in the tundra where the danger from mosquitos and flies to the newly-born deer is reduced. In Finland there are also some wild reindeer, the rangifer tarandus fennicus. The small number still remaining live mostly in the northernmost part of the country and of Russia, but recently the central-western territory in the area of Reisjärvi and Perho has been successfully repopulated.

culture, the Scandinavian countries founded the Sami Scandinavian Institute in 1973, while the Nordic Council of the Sami was established in 1956; as a consequence of this opening, the Sami language is now accepted as legal idiom in schools and courts.

In the wild territories of northeastern Lapland too, there are plenty of examples of the composite culture and original workmanship of the Lapps. In **Posio** we can find the products of Lapp-style ceramic work. Traditional forms and colours have today merged with more modern designs, giving rise to completely original works. The small town of **Salla**, on the other hand, is completely dedicated to the reindeer and its associations. Here there is the **Reindeer Park (Poropuisto)** where all the economic activities linked to the

animal are exhaustively portrayed – and it is also possible to go for a ride on a reindeer.

Among the most interesting places from the point of view of local handicrafts is **Kemijärvi**, the last city of any size in northern Finland. It is here that the real Sami territory begins, and this is the entrance to the territory famous for its gold-seeking and forth renowned Arctic Way, which thousands of Europeans travel every year in order to reach the Nordkapp, the northernmost point of the continent of Europe. Every year there are various events, among them the International Week of Sculpture, in which Lapp and foreign artists take part. The goods produced in the previous year are permanently displayed. The town of **Sodankylä**, already a gathering point for the Lapps in the sixteenth century, is

important from the point of view of Lapp art; one of its most important exponents is Andreas Alariesto, whose paintings are displayed in the gallery bearing his name. The city is also wellknown because in June the International Cinema event known as the **Midnight Sun Film Festival** is held there.

However, the most popular Lapp painter is certainly **Reidar Särestöniemi**. His birthplace is in **Kittilä** and it has been transformed into a museum. The most striking feature of his paintings is the uniqueness and vivid colours of the northern landscape, which seem almost to emerge from the paintings and enwrap us.

In the first days of September there is also a marathon in this little town; since it is organised each year, it is probably the most northerly annual event in the world.

The landscape of the tundra in Lapland.

As we continue to head north, not far from the village of **Pokka**, on **Lake Taatsi**, a great rock in the form of a column can be seen. Known as the **Taatsin seita**, it was considered a sacred place by the Sami people, a kind of dwelling-place for their gods.

Inari, with its seventeen thousand square kilometres, is the biggest municipal area in Finland, but also the least densely inhabited. It is also the real heartland of Lapp culture. Here and at **Sevettijärvi**, the village which faces on to the northern shores of the lake, about two thousand Lapps live, five hundred of whom belong to the S*kolt* ethnic group, orthodox in religion, who until 1944 lived in the city of Petsamo, which now belongs to Russia. They speak three languages, Russian and Skolt, as well as Finnish.

In Inari one can visit the **Sami Open-air Museum**, which provides a broad over-view of the culture and way of life of this ethnic group. In a thick pine forest, the last permanent homes of the Lapps which remained after the second world war have been collected together, and here it is possible to find the hand-made craft goods with typical Sami decoration, using materials gathered directly from nature, and especially from the reindeer. Traditional costumes and hunting and fishing implements are also on display.

Another important meeting-point for the Sami is the **Erämaakirkko** near Lake Pielpajärvi, seven kilometres from Inari. The atmosphere which surrounds this church, in the midst of the wild Lapland countryside, is of a quiet solemnity. The area around the church has been a point of exchange and trade over the centuries for these people, who have held their market there since the first church was built in 1646. The present building dates from 1760, and a number of subsequent restorations have returned the paintings near the pulpit to their original splendour.

Lake Inari, with its three thousand islands, is another important site for the Sami. The **Island of Ukko** (or A*jjih* in Samian language, can be reached by boat; it has been a sanctuary for at least a thousand years.

A view of the Tenojoki river, near Utsjoki.

LAPLAND BETWEEN SWEDEN AND NORWAY

The city of **Tornio** in Finnish Lapland makes a pair with the Swedish city of **Haparanda**, but although there is a boundary between them on the map, in reality they form a single city, each part closely linked to the other.

Tornio has one of the most beautiful wooden churches in Finland, dating from 1686, but the main attractions of the town are its setting and its sporting facilities. One example for many: the city's great **Kukkolankoski Rapids**. These are more than three kilometres long, and the difference in level is around 45 feet. Every year the spectacular Arctic Canoing Regatta is held on these rapids.

One curious feature is that the *Green Zone* Golf Course has its eighteen holes divided between Finland and Sweden, between which there is a time difference of an hour!

Heading North again, we come to the city of **Ylitornio,** again on the border with Sweden, which also has its Swedish twin, **Övertorneå**. The city is a well-known tourist resort, since it stands near the **Aavasaksa** mountains, on the summit of which the traditional *Midsummer Night's Festival* is held at the end of June each year.

Another village on the Swedish boundary is **Pello**, situated on the banks of the river which marks the actual frontier: on the other bank is the usual Swedish twin town, to which Pello is united by a bridge. The name of Pello is associated above all with salmon fishing, and with the **Poikkinainti Festival**, which takes place every July and celebrates marriages along the frontier with great festivities. Every year there is an actual marriage ceremony in the middle of the town's river, followed by traditional singing and dancing.

The village of **Kolari**, hidden away in the typical Nordic landscape of the border country, and the last railway station in the north of Finland, is near the winter sports centre of **Ylläs Tunturi**, 2350 feet high, where the longest downward ski-slopes of Finland are found.

Near here there is another place sacred to the Lapps: **Pakasaivo**, the Lapland Hell, where the ancestors of the present-day Lapps used to make sacrifices to their deities. It is a lake hidden away in a forest, the surface of which is around 150 feet below ground level.

Further north again is **Muonio**, where a short walk across the Muonionjoki Bridge brings one into Sweden. The city was already inhabited during the Stone Age, and today it is a focal point for the whole area of north-eastern Lapland. The wooden **Church** was designed in 1817 by an Italian architect, Carlo Bassi. Close at hand is the beautiful lake Jerisjärvi, where some fishermen's cottages dating from the eighteenth century are still in a good state of preservation.

Sweden can also be reached very easily from the village of **Kaaresuvanto** and its twin town, **Karesuando**. From both villages it is possible to see the midnight sun from the middle of July onwards.

Kilpisjärvi, on the lake of the same name, is the first village that one meets with in the triple frontier area between Sweden, Norway and Finland. From the city, Mount Saana can be seen, more than 3500 feet high, and surrounded with magnificent countryside. Another frontier post between Norway and Finland is **Karigasniemi**, on the river Tenojoki. The whole area is a mythical zone for the Lapps, and the view from nearby Mount Ailigas is absolutely superb.

Again on the Norwegian border, we find **Utsjoki**, the major attraction of which is the **Kevo Canyon**, 40 kilometres in length. The most beautiful part of the gorge is where the river Kevojoki opens into the long and narrow Lake Njaggaljärvi, a scene which can only be reached by foot, but is every bit worth the effort.

HISTORICAL NOTES

The territory which we call Finland today first became inhabited immediately after the last Ice Age. The ethnic group which settled there devoted its life to hunting and fishing, and belonged to the Ugro-Finnish family, originating from the Ural area, the Baltic, and the territory where Karelia is today. The various tribes of the Karelians, Estonians and Finns also encountered the Sami people on this territory, and were scattered throughout the whole territory of Finland, but especially along the coast.

However, these Finnish lands did not form any kind of a national entity until the twelfth century, when both Sweden and the Catholic Church on the one hand, and Russia and the Orthodox Church on the other, began to take an interest in them. Thus the peoples of the more westerly regions developed closer ties with the west, while Karelia and the surrounding zones were more influenced by Russia and Byzantium.

In 1216 Pope Innocent III awarded this territory to the Kings of Sweden, who continued the work of penetration into Finland, both from the religious and the military standpoints, until they were forced to halt not far from Karelia. At this point, in 1323, after a series of clashes with the Russians, a peace was signed whereby Sweden and the autonomous Russian principality of Novgorod divided the territory between them: eastern Karelia going to Novgorod, and western and southern Finland being integrated into the Swedish context, though with parity of rights.

The most important city in Finland at that time was Turku (founded in the 13th century), which assumed the role of capital.

Later, for more than a century (1617 – 1721) Sweden enjoyed a period of enormous power, and Finland was the scene of the majority of Sweden's military undertakings in that era. However, despite the fact that the official language was Swedish, Finnish culture in its own right found it possible to make significant developments, especially after the opening of the first Finnish University at Turku in 1640.

Sweden's great power, however, suffered severe setbacks during the Northern Wars of 1700 – 1721. With Sweden engaged in fighting on the European front, the Russians took the opportunity of occupying Finland, the south-western part of which was ceded to them by the Swedes in 1712. This period is remembered as the days of "the great hatred", and is compared to the other period known as "the little hatred", in which during the subsequent wars between Russia and Sweden (1741 – 1743), the Finnish/Swedish army was defeated, and Finland lost yet more territory, which passed to the Russia of the Empress Anna, and Catherine the Great.

In 1806 Sweden, which joined the coalition against Napoleon, gave Czar Alexander I the opportunity to take possession of the whole of Finland, defeated and occupied from 1808 onward. This time the peace treaty between Russia and Finland finally acknowledged the passage of Finland under the Russian Imperial government – an important strategic conquest for the new rulers, especially in relation to the defence of the city of St Petersburg.

Finland, now an autonomous Grand Duchy of the Russian Empire, had been assured by the Czar that he would undertake to respect its Lutheran Evangelical faith and its constitutional laws. The Czar granted many favours to the country in order to diminish the influence that Sweden still possessed there. The capital was brought nearer to Russia; transferred to Helsinki, it was rebuilt in magnificent fashion to make it worthy of its new function.

Finland's autonomy brought with it a significant growth in the feeling of national identity. It is from this

period that the Kalevala dates, the poem written by Elias Lönnrot, which celebrated the nation's saga, while the patriotic poetry of Runeberg stirred up Finnish spirits, animating them with a renewed and stronger national sentiment.

It was during the reign of Alexander III that the Russians began to show signs of anxiety about the growing organisation of nationalist movements, and as a result, an attrition of Finnish autonomy began, eventually resulting in serious oppression. The rebellions and defeats of Russia on various fronts, such as Japan, finally led Czar Nicholas II to liberalise the Finnish government, which in 1906 put into effect one of the most revolutionary parliamentary reforms of the age: the one-chamber parliament was elected on the basis of direct universal suffrage, and women obtained the vote in political elections, and full effective political rights – the first European women to do so.

However, Russia did not give up so easily, and there was a second period of oppression, which lasted until 1914. The events of the Russian Revolution of 1917, however, enabled Finland to return to the institutional liberties it had gained previously. It was only during the First World War that Finland declared itself independent, in 1917. The war contributed to the liberation of Finland from the Russian troops who still remained in the country, and Finland's independence was recognised by the new Russian government in 1918.

the years between the wars, nland's political situation moved the right, as a virtual reaction inst the events which in that iod were affecting the new et Union. In the thirties, the try established important links Nazi Germany, something clearly did not escape notice. He considered as a vital point for the of the Leningrad area and tern Baltic against the nist aims of Hitler. In this Stalin claimed the right to rritories of Karelia and to

certain military bases along the coast. Finland's firm refusal led to a Russian invasion in 1939, forcing the Finns to fight a very hard and bitter war, known as the Winter War, which ended in 1940 with the Peace of Moscow. On that occasion, the country lost the isthmus of Karelia and the naval base of Hanko.

There was another moment of grave uncertainty over Finland's fate in the so-called War of Continuation (1941), when Finland chose to ally with Germany in the pursuit of the second world war. Going beyond the former borders of Karelia in the course of the war, the Finnish army remained there until 1944, the year in which the Russian counter-offensive forced the Finns to sign an armistice which returned the frontier situation to that previously established in 1940. But this time, Finland was forced to yield the region of Lapland known as Petsamo.

At the Peace of Paris in 1947, the Moscow armistice was ratified, but the surrender on lease to the Soviet Union of the region of Porkkala, near Helsinki, was also sanctioned, and heavy war reparations were also imposed, which the country paid punctually in the specified time, a unique case among the countries penalised in this way.

In 1955 Finland became a member of the United Nations and the Nordic Council, and has adopted a neutralist policy which has led it to play a role in numerous diplomatic initiatives. In 1973 it signed a free trade agreement with what was then the European Common Market, and at the moment it enjoys friendly relations with all the European nations, fostering its diplomatic, commercial and cultural contacts with them.

Since January 1995, Finland has been a member of the European Union.

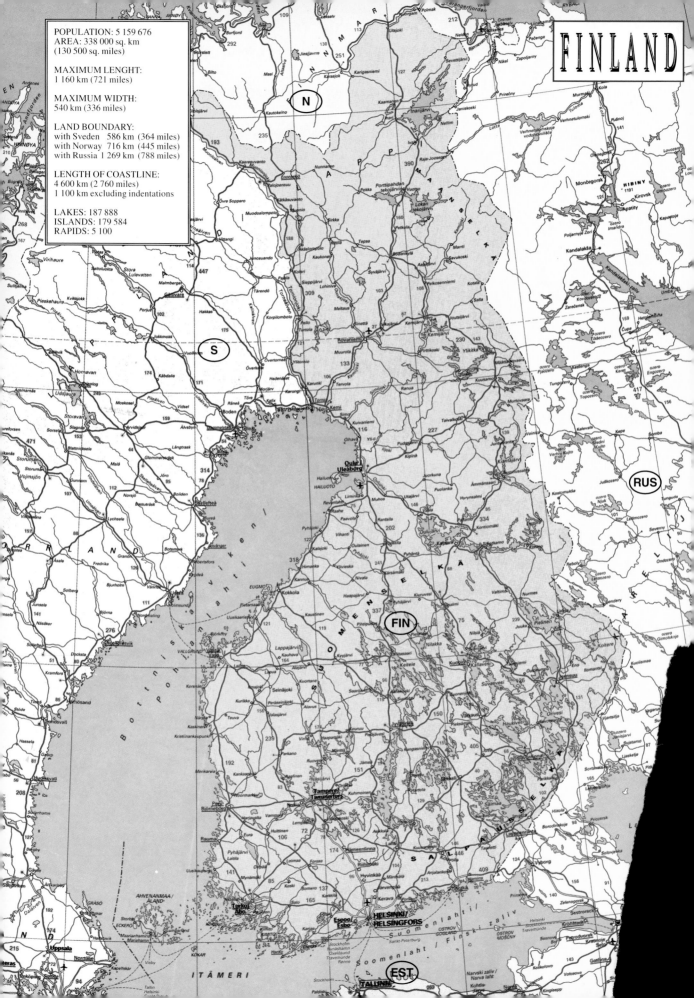